HOW TO HAVE A FINANCIAL HEART ATTACK

Book Design by HMDPublishing.com

CONTENTS

THE PENNY CANDY FOUNDATION

IT all started in my childhood. Receiving a weekly allowance, a whopping 10 bucks a week for chores: keeping my room clean, washing dishes, even though my legs would burn from standing in place so long, or at least that was the excuse that I'd tell my parents. Cleaning my bathroom. I didn't mind wiping the mirrors, wiping the sink, sweeping, and even cleaning the tub. But the amount of time it took to convince myself to clean my toilet seemed to take an act of Congress. The amount of Ajax and Scrubbing Bubbles I used to clean the inside and outside of the bowl seemed to disappear. I would wear that toilet wire handle scrubber out. I would imagine that I was sword fighting. Yes, I had a big imagination. The amount of chemicals floating around, I'm surprised I never fainted.

But here's where the financial heart attack begins, right in my childhood bedroom. See, I didn't know it then, but that 10-dollar bill was teaching me the most dangerous lesson of my life: money will always come. Every single Friday, like clockwork, that crisp bill would appear. It didn't matter if I'd blown last week's allowance on Now and Laters and video games. It didn't matter if I had nothing left by Tuesday. Friday was coming, and Friday meant money.

This is how I would go broke immediately. On Sunday after church, shoutout to Mt. Zion, on Washington Rd in High Point. After my mother, who was an Evangelist, would watch me like an eagle staring at its prey because I was known to fall asleep on the back pew surrounded by my friends. If I went to sleep, I couldn't go to the penny candy store 3 doors down from the church. This would feel like the worst punishment ever to a kid. Yes, there were numerous occasions when I didn't make it to the store due to bad behavior.

But back to the story, me and the crew would stroll over and buy penny candy, yes you heard me correctly. It literally was a penny a piece. I know this generation will never experience these glorified penny prices. As I sit here and write, I think about those days and ask, 'Inflation, where?' In addition to the brown bag full of delicious candy, this store had video games. Galaga, Ms. Pac-Man, and my all-time favorite was Pole Position. This is where the competition would begin. It had an actual steering wheel, and you would race in a formula-type scenario. The biggest surprise was that all video games cost a quarter - yes, I said one quarter.

We would line up and drive one by one. Those were some of the best days of my life. I would blow my entire 10 bucks because I had no concept of saving or the 4-quadrant method or anything. My child-size brain could only conceive that by doing my chores, I would receive a fresh new $10 bill next Friday, like clockwork. This repeated behavior stuck in my head. This muscle memory, this financial amnesia, this belief that money is infinite as long as you show up, it's the same mentality that would cost me tens of thousands of dollars in my twenties and thirties. But we'll get to that.

THE BLUEPRINT I IGNORED

MY mother was an Evangelist and a small business owner. She ran a pretty successful daycare with nothing but an 8th-grade education. My father was very hardworking, often serving as a supervisor at most of his jobs, which were in factories that required physical labor. I know they would discuss finances and budgeting, and before making any major purchases, they'd talk and bring out the financial college rule notebook. They'd write the vision and make it plain. Habakkuk 2:2. And they would pray about it, and even, depending on the purchase, make a few changes to the figures.

I remember my parents trying to explain finances and keep records. I would listen and try to focus, but as you guessed, it went in one ear and out the other. I even remember my parents keeping every receipt. I didn't understand at first, but my mother had a business accountant, and sometimes I'd go with her to his house. Tall gentleman, brown skinned with glasses and a very deep voice, reminds you of The Temptations singing the Christmas song Silent Night.

Looking back now, I had the blueprint right in front of me. Two parents who came from nothing, built something, and managed it wisely. But you know what they say about wisdom? It's wasted on those who aren't ready to receive it. I wasn't ready. I was too busy planning my next trip to the penny candy store, my next quarter in Pole Position, my next weekend adventure.

THE FIRST PAYCHECK SYNDROME

BACK to the story, my first job was at Columbia Food Mart. I was a bagger, I think I was making around 7 dollars an hour, and you could get snacks on your break, and they would keep tabs of your daily purchases by writing your name on your receipts. So at the end of the week, your purchases would be deducted from our weekly checks. By now, I'm 15 years old, and I still have the mindset of spending everything I make, because I know I will get another paycheck next week.

I would have conversations with my parents about saving money, but all I could think of was Lamont Donta McLeod in that moment in that very place. I was never thinking about 30 years from now. Some of those same negative, negligent traits would still loom in my mental space. One thing is certain: most preteens, teens, and young adults don't think about 30-40 years in the future or plan for or create generational wealth. We are only interested in Friday and Saturday nights. This is the extent of our financial healthcare.

But here's what I didn't understand at 15: I was building a financial identity. Every time I cashed that check and spent it all, I was telling my brain, 'This is who you are. This is what you do with money.' I was programming myself for poverty disguised as fun. And the scary part? It felt good. It felt right. It felt like freedom.

Think about it like this: if you practice basketball every day for a year, you get better at basketball. If you practice piano every day for a year, you get better at piano. Well, I was practicing being broke every day for years. I was getting really, really good at it. I was developing expertise in financial failure. And just like any skill you practice long enough, it becomes automatic. It becomes who you are.

I remember one specific Friday at Columbia Food Mart. I'd gotten my check, $98 after they deducted my snack purchases for the week. I had $98 in my hand, and you know what I felt? Rich. Powerful. Like I could do anything. By Sunday night, I had $3. Three dollars. And you know what I felt? Nothing. I felt nothing. Because in my mind, next Friday was coming. Next Friday would bring another $98. The cycle would repeat. Forever.

That's the trap. That's the invisible cage. When you believe money is infinite, you never learn to value it. When you believe there's always more coming, you never learn to protect what you have. When you believe Friday will save you, you never learn to save yourself.

SPRING BREAK 1997: MY FIRST REAL FINANCIAL HEART ATTACK

FAST forward. I remember attending spring break my senior year in high school. Myself and a few of my friends and cousins went down to Myrtle Beach, South Carolina. We found a house to rent, and yes, this was way before Airbnb, so I have no idea how my cousin came across this place. However, he booked it, we all pooled our money together, and we hit the road for a week of fun in the sun.

Wait, you asked how I funded this trip? I was working, managed to save 2 paychecks, and borrowed some funds from my parents. Because this was long before Zelle and CashApp, so basically what you took with you was basically all you were going to have until you returned back home.

Let's discuss my first financial error in this scenario. Typically, not saying in all cases, most times when you borrow money from your parents, there are no guidelines, no rules on the return payment method, it's not written down anywhere. Hence, it's not legally bonded, there are no penalties for missed payments, there are no interest rates, default clauses, etc. Basically, what you hear is Don't forget that you owe me money. With a smile on your face, you seem to think that you've won some type of fictitious victory. But boy oh boy, you'll find out how you are setting yourself up to have a financial heart attack in years to come.

This right here, this is where the disease spread. When you borrow without consequences, you learn that debt is soft. You learn that money you don't have is still money you can spend. You learn that the future you will figure it out, because the present you have more important things to worry about, like whether you're going to the beach or not.

Anyways, back to this epic boys' trip to Myrtle Beach, South Carolina. My parents had a 1993 Buick Roadmaster. It was a beautiful hunter green, and in my true Pops fashion, he wasn't driving anything until he had whitewall tires. Not just any whitewalls but Royal Seals. They had a gold stripe and the white wall. My parents drove nice cars because they knew how to budget and plan.

Back to the story, there were a couple of cars following each other down the highway because Pops' number 1 rule was don't have a carload of your friends in my car. He would say, 'If I ever catch you with a carload, I'm going to make them walk and you.' I didn't want to test this theory, so I kept it to 2 at max 3 of us in the car, per my father's threats.

What are the essentials you need when traveling? Did you mention gas? You are correct, and you need a lot of it. Even though gas was only 1 dollar and change back in the 90s, it's still a lot when you are a broke teenager with no clue what financial literacy looked like until it smacked you in the face. What else do you need on road trips? What did you say over there in the back row, snacks and food? You got that right. One thing I can tell you for sure is that teenage boys can put away some food and a lot of it.

We finally arrived at sunny, beautiful Myrtle Beach, South Carolina. At that time, it was the only beach I had traveled to, so you could not tell me there was a more beautiful beach in the world. It was only 3 hours from my hometown of High Point, North Carolina; it literally was heaven on earth. We unpacked our vehicles, select our rooms, and, as you might guess, we head to the strip.

There was nothing like the strip of Myrtle Beach; you could ride or walk for miles and miles. Watching the beautiful girls from all over. For myself and the rest of the delegation from spring break 1997 in Myrtle Beach. Thank God there were no social media platforms around during those years. I think that part is self-explanatory.

Every day you eat out for breakfast, lunch, and dinner, and snacks in between when you are running the streets all day. I didn't care what year it was; that gets expensive in any economy. You would think that I would have known that a financial heart attack was coming, the way I was big spending. For 7 days in a row, with no parental guidelines and no one to ask for advice or guide me financially, how do you think I fared financially? Yes, you guessed it, broke as a joke with no room to choke.

You know that natural high you feel the day you leave for vacation? The endorphins are released, and you need and want that day, or that ride down, or that feeling to never end. Well, buttercup, once you come down, and it is the end of the trip, and it's time to pack the car, clean up all the mess you made at the beach house, and pray you didn't damage too much, so you get your deposit back. You realize you are flat broke, and that's no joke.

But the worst part wasn't being broke. The worst part was that little voice in the back of my head that said, 'Worth it.' That's the voice that kills dreams. That's the voice that keeps people in financial bondage for decades. Because if you believe every dollar spent on temporary pleasure is worth it, you'll never save a dollar for permanent security.

THE JOB HOPPING HUSTLE

YOU would think that after my childhood, not saving, not learning the importance of saving for the future, surely the first job I'd have a clue about saving money, investing, money market, stock markets, or IULs or something. Clearly, you weren't following closely enough, because boy, oh boy, does it get much worse.

I graduated from high school, 'Go Cowboy Nation' class of 1997. After graduating from high school, I continued to exhibit the same negative, financially negligent traits. I had a choice made by my parents. Either attend college or go to work. Of course, I opted to go to work; I just didn't think college was the right fit for me.

I worked as a clothing packer at Polo Ralph Lauren. My manager had the Porsche and designer clothing. He was making the money and living the lifestyle I desired, but I lacked the financial literacy and patience to achieve that goal at the time. I wanted to cut corners and get rich fast. Now I look back and realize that, in most cases, when you get rich quickly, you lose it even quicker. Still wanted to live for the weekend. No savings, no real financial plans or goals, because I knew I'd get another check next week.

Of course, I didn't listen to my manager and supervisors. I wanted to do things my way and on my own time. Yes, you guessed it, they finally got fed up with my behavior and fired me. Mr. Nonchalant didn't care because I had a masterful ability to land good jobs but lacked what it took to grow in the space to fully capitalize on the moment.

Out of a job, meaning I had to borrow gas money from my parents, but it was contingent upon my not taking any trips or shopping. It was strictly to find another job. I eventually landed a job at Volvo Trucking in their accounting department. I was magical with numbers, but had no clue how to take money to grow money. I thought success was tied to working a lot of hours and blowing my entire check. Yes, this was a recipe for disaster.

Here's what nobody tells you about being good at getting jobs but bad at keeping them: you're training yourself to stay at the bottom. Every time you start over, you reset your earning potential, your benefits, and your advancement opportunities. You're running on a financial treadmill, burning calories but going nowhere.

BLACK BIKE WEEK AND BORROWED TIME

MY cousins and I took another trip to Black Bike Week at Myrtle Beach, South Carolina. Remember, I just landed this new job and had no PTO or vacation time because I had only been there a very short amount of time. I took a chance and took the days off anyway, hoping and praying I had a job when I returned.

Little money, no savings, I just took a week's check and joined my cousins at the beach. It was definitely one for the history books. We had an amazing time. Blowing money I really didn't have. Someone went to jail, so we had to pool our money together and get them out of jail before our parents found out.

After this wild and crazy adventure, I was broke as a joke, barely enough money to gas up my car and make it back to High Point, North Carolina. I went to work as if I didn't miss a few days the previous week. Gave an elaborate excuse, and my supervisor bought it hook, line, and sinker.

Of course, I still had the toxic traits of doing what I wanted to do and not following the instructions of upper management, so you guessed it. I was eventually fired. Back out of a job yet again, I had to borrow money from my parents with hopes of finding another job, and no traveling and no shopping.

You would think that, having been fired from all my previous jobs and not saving money, nor thinking about my future or a rainy day, that I would be thinking, acting, and moving differently. Let's just see how this goes.

This cycle, right here, this is what I call the financial heart attack treadmill. You're moving, you're sweating, your heart is racing, but you're not going anywhere. And the worst part? You think you're okay because you keep landing new jobs. You confuse employment with financial health. They're not the same thing. Not even close.

THE GAS COMPANY GETAWAY

REMEMBER, I told you that I was gifted in the sense that I landed a good job because I interviewed very well, and I have always been a fast thinker and witty with my responses and wordplay. Here goes nothing, I landed a job at Piedmont Natural Gas in High Point. I was a gas meter reader. This was the perfect job because I had a company vehicle, which meant I didn't have to buy gas, and I could rack up the mileage. The best part was that I wasn't confined to a cubicle. Shoutout to my cubicle nation, no disrespect to you for what you do and the genius work you produce, I just know that cubicle life wasn't for me.

I trained for 2 weeks with my supervisor, who was a very cool gentleman. He took me out, showed me the ropes on how to read the meters and run my route, and the biggest gem he showed me was that if you finished your route early, you would still get paid for a full day. You have no idea how sweet that sounds to a slacker. It's literally a dream come true.

I remember one of our training sessions. We went to a rural area, and I was terrified of dogs. Still am to this day, yet my children currently have 3 dogs, go figure. Back to the story, we pulled up to a home with a large fence around it, and I heard barking. Of course, I was wishing the dogs were next door, but you guessed it, they ran to the fence as soon as we turned off our truck.

I moved very slowly and hesitated, hoping he'd say You stay back, and I'll get this one but those words he never uttered. He said, 'Come with me, you'd be surprised how many homes have dogs. It doesn't stop us from doing our job because each meter on our route must be read.'

These were the largest 4 dogs I've ever seen in my life. They leaned up against the fence, and their combined weight had the fence leaning to the point where they could have jumped over if they chose to do so. Thankfully, they did not, and we proceeded to go and do our job. I remember, like it was yesterday, the dogs ran up to us and truthfully had a playful demeanor. My supervisor stuck his hand out and rubbed his fingers together, and said, 'Hey sugar' and proceeded to rub the dog's head as they licked his hand. I almost fainted at the amount of saliva coming from their mouths. He made them feel very comfortable, and we proceeded to read the meter and move on to the next house.

Do you feel like every time I get a new job, a vacation is attached to it? Well, if you did, you would be correct. This was March of 1999, and my cousin came up with the great idea for us to travel to Atlanta, Georgia, for a world-renowned event called 'Freaknik.'

FREAKNIK 1999: THE ATLANTA AWAKENING

WE packed our bags, loaded up in 2 vehicles, and hopped on 85S headed to the Black Mecca, Atlanta, GA. Do you think I was prepared financially? Do you think I'd learned from my previous jobs and lessons to have saved money for this trip or for the future? Surely you didn't think I matured financially, and you would be correct. I had a nice paycheck. We were splitting gas and hotel fare, so I felt like I was on top of the world for this trip.

We arrived in Atlanta, and the traffic was bumper-to-bumper. I had been to huge events before, and I didn't think it could get any better than a homecoming experience of North Carolina A&T in the 90s, which is now called 'GHOE', which means Greatest Homecoming On Earth. Yes, it was that epic.

I had never been to a place where the entire city was a party. This was the pinnacle of parties. We didn't book a room; we didn't really know anything about Atlanta, so we didn't know where to stay. We winged it as per usual. Funny story, anytime we traveled to a new city, we'd always ask where is Martin Luther King Drive. Because unfortunately, this is almost always located in the hood, and that's where we wanted to be, because that's where the fun was.

We partied in the parking lot of the famous Club 112 on Cheshire Bridge Road. We had so much fun that first night, it really changed the trajectory of my life. We finally made it to a motel that definitely didn't look safe or savory. I was terrified, but everyone else was down, so I went with the crowd. I didn't know if I'd ever prayed that much in my life for our safety. It was very cheap, so it was a win for us.

To give you a glimpse of how sketchy this motel was, this guy saw us check in and noticed our North Carolina plates. When you're not from somewhere, folks who live in that area know that you are not a native to that area because of the way you act, talk, dress, and carry yourself. I'll never forget what he said: 'I hope you fellas are ready for the show tonight; it's going to go down.' We all looked at each other and shrugged our shoulders, and proceeded to unpack.

We kept running into this guy, and each time he would say I hope you fellas are ready for tonight because it's going down. Y'all, I promise you aren't ready for what I'm getting ready to tell you because I couldn't believe it, and I witnessed it with my own eyes. This lady came knocking on the door, and we opened it. She came in and said Who's buying because I'm selling fantasies. I literally almost choked because I had never experienced anything like this in my teenage life. We told her no, and she said thank you and went and knocked on the next door. We laughed and talked about what just happened, and proceeded to hang out.

Of course, the next day, we basically blew all of our money, and if you were thinking, 'Did they have enough money for a motel room the next night?' we didn't, so we had to sleep in the car. Definitely wasn't my proudest moment, but what can I say, it happened. We woke up that Sunday morning, gassed up, and jumped back on 85N heading to High Point, North Carolina.

If you thought sleeping in the car was bad, as soon as we crossed into the North Carolina state line, my friend's car broke down at exit 95. I think about that to this day, each time I travel to North Carolina. Back to the story, we didn't have any money for a tow truck, and I had to break down and call my parents to come and pick us up, 2 and a half hours away.

I was so embarrassed to have to call my parents, yet forever grateful for the fact that, without hesitation, my parents came to pick us up. When my mom and dad arrived, I didn't get fussed at immediately, but boy, did I get an earful after we dropped my cousin and friend off at their houses. I got fussed at for going broke, fussed at for not being financially prepared. I got fussed at for the old and the new.

But here's what stuck with me from that ride home. My father said something I'll never forget: 'Son, being broke is a choice you keep making over and over again.' At the time, I thought he was just being hard on me. Now I know he was trying to save me from myself.

Back to reality and work. I was finally on my own, reading meters, and 3 days into my first solo week, I was in a backyard reading a meter, and the cutest little dog came around the corner barking. I guess I didn't show him any fear, so he left and came back moments later with a bigger dog. When that bigger dog barked, it felt like my soul shook, and all I could think to do was run.

When I cranked up this big block Chevy I was running, I was running. Don't let anyone fool you into thinking fat people can't run. Scare them bad enough, and you'll see record-breaking speed. I remember passing the front door of the house and I remember the lady saying, 'Sir please don't run, my dogs don't bite' I didn't care nothing about what she was saying, I was on the way to the company's truck.

I got in, caught my breath, and went home, where I told my mother about the incident. She said something magical. Take those people their truck; you don't have to go through that. You can find another job. I think I skipped to the company truck, drove back to Piedmont Natural Gas, parked the truck, went inside, turned in my keys, and left without explanation.

THE ATLANTA DECISION

I GOT back home and waited for my father to get off work, and called a family meeting. I said I know you gave me a choice of going to work or going to college. I said I tried it my way and wasn't successful, so I beg of you, please let me go to college. They said they'd think about it and let me know.

When I was in Atlanta, I picked up an apartment guide because I wanted to move to Atlanta. They finally came back and said, 'Okay, you can apply to schools.' I immediately told them that I wanted to move to Atlanta and attend school. My mother, God rest her soul, immediately said No way, no how, that's too far. My option was community college or North Carolina A&T.

As much fun as I had at Aggie Nation, it was nothing in comparison to my weekend in Atlanta. I begged and pleaded my case, but I kept getting denied until we took a family trip that summer of 1999 to New Jersey and New York to visit family. Every vehicle tag we passed on the highway, I'd say there goes Atlanta. That's where I want to attend school.

Can you imagine hearing this for 9 hours straight, every car we passed from North Carolina to Virginia through DC, Maryland, Delaware, and New Jersey. 85N to 95N to 495 to 95N and on the turnpike of New Jersey? My father was completely sick of hearing it all the way there and back, and eventually said We're going to make sure you move to Atlanta, and the responsibility of staying is on you. You want to be a man, we're going to treat you like one.

And with that nod from my father, I began looking at colleges in the Atlanta, Georgia area. I stumbled upon DeVry University. It had an

Accounting Information Systems program. I had a gift with numbers that my Accounting teacher from high school said I really should look at going to school for Accounting, and that's where the seed was planted, watered, and nurtured. I really appreciate what my Accounting teacher saw in me, and all I'll say to my family reading this is make sure the dreams you pursue are actually your dreams. In my humble opinion, I feel you will put more effort, blood, sweat, and tears into what you want to come to fruition. Just my 2 cents.

Anyways, I submitted my application and loan applicants, grants, etc., honestly not having any idea what I was really doing. I just knew my path to Atlanta was enrolling in college. As time passed, I began searching for an apartment. I honestly was manifesting even before I fully understood what I was doing. As I look back, I learned that I was far ahead of my time, just wasted too much time trying to cut corners and live for the weekend, and not plan for the future.

Remember, I told you that I picked up an apartment book while we visited Atlanta during Freaknik. Again, there is no real plan, and I have no idea how to properly research apartments, neighborhoods, crime rates, demographics, etc. I just wanted to move to the A-Town. Here was my process. I literally looked in an apartment guidebook and seriously only looked for places with cheap rent.

I stumbled upon an apartment in College Park on Washington Rd, and at that time, it was called Azalea Manor. I didn't visit, walk the grounds, check the location; I simply decided that for $400 a month, this was going to be my new home as long as I was accepted into DeVry University.

For the first time in my life, I actually put forth a real effort to save money and prepare for my big move to Atlanta. I have finally received my acceptance letter from DeVry University, and I am pleased to have been accepted. I shared the good news with my parents, and my father's response was Well, you did your part and got accepted, so now it's our turn, and we'll assist you with the move.

My mother wasn't happy at all about the fact that I was leaving North Carolina for Atlanta, but she eventually understood it was time for me to step out on my own. Let me give you this timeline. It was March of 1999 when we attended Freaknik and applied for college and were accepted, found an apartment, and moved in by November 6th of 1999. A lot can happen in 6 months if you really apply yourself and have real support.

MOVING DAY AND NEW BEGINNINGS

BACK story, I remember telling my friends that I was moving to Atlanta, and I didn't think they believed me until they came down my parents' street and saw the U-Haul with my convertible strapped down on the car hauler. It was a funny conversation with them. I remember them saying, 'Wow, you really are moving,' and I laughed and told them that I was addicted to Atlanta after Freaknik, and I had to move there.

I remember I had a custom-made sectional, which we picked up before the trip down. We hit 85S and were Atlanta-bound. I couldn't sleep a wink, I was so excited. I drove my dad's 1993 Buick Roadmaster following close behind my parents in the U-Haul. We finally arrived in College Park, Georgia.

There was a security guard at the gate, and each visitor had to stop, show their ID, and provide the apartment number they were visiting. We told him we were going to the office because I was moving in. He granted us access, and we proceeded to drive to the leasing office. I remember driving over the few speed bumps and looking around at the apartment buildings and cars leading up to the leasing office. We parked and walked inside.

Remember, I'd never been there before, so my parents and I saw my new residence at the same time. The lady in the office was friendly, and we went over the leasing agreement. We also gave her my deposit, which I still have the receipt for to this day. She handed me my keys to my new apartment, and we walked over to my new place, which was apartment 15-2E.

We walked up and I placed the key and turned the lock and low and behold I was home. I walked in, and it had a step down as you entered through the front door, leading directly into the living room. If you kept walking, there was my kitchen on the left through the living room. We walked back around, and down the hallway was my bathroom on the left, and then you would walk straight into my bedroom. I was so proud and excited about my 1-bedroom and 1-bath apartment.

We walked the leasing agent to the door and shook her hand, thanking her for everything that had been seamless up to that point. After we closed the door in true my mother's fashion, she prayed over my new apartment. In each room, the kitchen, bathroom, and living room, etc., my mother was a praying woman, may God rest her soul.

After praying, it was time to walk back to the leasing office and get the vehicles, and begin the unloading process. We had a deep conversation walking back to the U-Haul, and it's one I'll never forget. It was about growing up and the importance of being cautious, aware of my surroundings, and praying for my protection as I was in this new state and city all alone at the tender age of 19.

I'll never forget my father saying You are a man now, and it's time to step up. We believe in you, and we're very proud of you. One of our best talks ever. Needless to say, it was a long, mentally, physically, and emotionally challenging walk, but it was also powerful and impactful. Really put things in perspective for the road ahead.

As I watched my parents load up, it hit me that this was my home and my parents were heading back to North Carolina. I stood and watched my father's Buick Roadmaster turn the corner and fade out of sight. I didn't know if you ever watched the Friday movie, but I turned and ran, crying, with my knuckles dragging the ground like Red did when Deebo snatched the chain off his neck. I was devastated.

I can't lie, I cried for hours, and I called to check on my parents as they traveled back home. My dad said he was going to put my mom out of the car because she was crying so much, he thought they were going to drown in the car. Eventually, my tears dried up when I realized my parents didn't pass away; they just went home. That thought made me feel a great deal better.

Those first 3 nights were a struggle. I was scared, my apartment backed up to the woods, and at night it was pitch dark, and every 8 seconds a plane flew over my apartment because I lived by the airport. By night 4, I was so tired I had no choice but to go to sleep because I was exhausted. I did not have any fight left in me, so a burglar would have just robbed me blind anyway.

But here's what nobody tells you about that first night alone: it's not just about being scared of the dark or the neighborhood or the planes. It's about being scared of yourself. It's about lying in that empty apartment, in that empty bed, in that empty city, and wondering if you have what it takes. Not just to survive, but to succeed. Not just to make it through the month, but to make something of your life.

I had $400 rent. I had student loans piling up. I had utilities, food, gas, insurance, phone bill, and a thousand other expenses I hadn't even thought about yet. And I was 19 years old with no real job, no real skills, and no real plan. Just a dream. Just ambition. Just a belief that somehow, some way, it would all work out.

You know what's funny? That belief, that faith, that blind optimism, it's both the best and worst thing about being young. It's what allows you to take risks, to chase dreams, to move to a new city with nothing but hope. But it's also what blinds you to reality, to consequences, to the mathematics of money. Because hope doesn't pay bills. Faith doesn't feed you. Optimism doesn't cover rent.

COLLEGE LIFE AND COLLECTIONS CALLS

BACK to how you have a financial heart attack. Starting college means taking on student loans, potentially leaving you up to your neck in debt before you even start class. You would think that, because I was going to school for Accounting Information Systems, that by now I would have at least a decent amount of knowledge when it came to balancing books, managing money, etc. Well, the survey says that you would be INCORRECT. I still had no clue.

My first job was at FNANB in Kennesaw, Georgia. It was a credit card collection agency. I found out very early that I had a knack for collections. God gifted me with a gift of gab, and I excelled very quickly. The hourly pay wasn't the best, but the commission structure is where I really shined. I worked part-time, but I was making full-time money.

I didn't have to pay my car payment or my insurance, which was a blessing. Although, as a 46-year-old man, I often ponder whether never really struggling financially, because if I fell short, my parents would bail me out, was a great thing or not. Please don't get me wrong; I was beyond thankful to have amazing parents whom I could call on in a financial pinch. But what does this really teach you? Nothing if you don't seize the moment and grow financially, and get to the point where you can stand on your own financially. Which, honestly, I didn't learn until many, many years later.

Unfortunately, even though I was making great money, the muscle memory I had as a child running to the penny candy store was still alive and well. I literally lived for the weekend. I was able to cover my basics, gas, food, utilities, and rent some of the time. As a college student, you are typically broke, but if you have no concept of financial literacy, it's much, much worse.

I lived paycheck to paycheck. I still had the mindset that it was a must to have the latest and greatest sneakers and clothes, just so I could look rich, but I was actually beyond poor because of my mindset. Thank God for praying parents; my utilities and rent were always paid, but I didn't pay on time. I essentially robbed Peter to pay Paul on a monthly basis.

And trying to keep up with dating multiple women is another financial nightmare waiting to happen. You can't grow taking out multiple women on multiple dates, yes, they would pay sometimes, which was great, but man, will this behavior keep you drowning in debt. It's so much I would say to my younger financial self but we'll get into that later.

Here's the irony that kills me looking back: I was calling people every day, professionally, asking them to pay their credit card bills. I was trained in payment arrangements, hardship programs, and the psychology of debt. I knew every excuse, every justification, every rationalization. And when I hung up that phone and clocked out? I went home and became the person I was calling. I was the debtor. I was the one behind on bills. I was the one making excuses. The teacher became the student in the worst way possible.

I'll never forget this one call. I was talking to a woman, maybe in her 40s, and she was crying. Literally crying on the phone. She said, 'I don't understand how this happened. I make good money. I have a good job. But every month I'm short. Every month, I'm struggling. Every month I tell myself this is the month I'll get ahead, and every month I fall further behind.'

I gave her the company speech. Set up a payment plan. Told her about our hardship program. Explained how she could get back on track. Professional. Efficient. Helpful. And then I hung up the phone, and I looked at my own bank account. $47. I had $47 to my name, and rent was due in 6 days. I was literally that woman. I was crying the same tears, just not on the phone with a collections agent. Yet.

The worst part? I knew better. That's what separates ignorance from stupidity. Ignorance is not knowing. Stupidity is knowing and doing it anyway. I was educated. I was trained. I understood concepts such as compound interest, payment schedules, credit scores, and financial planning. I could explain it all. I just couldn't do it. And that's the gap that destroys lives. The gap between knowing and doing. The gap between understanding and applying. The gap between theory and practice.

Every day at FNANB, I was collecting on people's mistakes. Every day, I was seeing the end result of bad financial decisions. Every day, I was talking to people who were 5, 10, 15 years older than me, living in the future I was creating for myself. And every day I clocked out and went right back to creating that future.

THE ROOMMATE LESSON

I LIVED on Washington Rd for 2 years, literally the best years of my young and dumb life. Eventually, I was fired from FNANB. I was totally the type you couldn't tell what to do, and because I thought I literally knew it all, and not being able to keep a job is yet another way to have a financial heart attack.

Remember, I was great at interviewing, so I landed another job almost immediately. Then, I told my parents I was fired once I safely secured my new job. I moved to Doraville, GA, and had a roommate that I knew from my old job. Mind you, because you and a person hang out together and seemingly agree on the same views, it doesn't mean you can live together, and boy, did I learn this the hard way.

I ran the idea by my parents, and they both said this was a horrible idea because roommates just don't work in most cases. This is where you find out things about people that you just don't want to know. My approach to my parents was Hey, this is great because I won't have to pay all the bills by myself, and I could save money, me and my roommate are basically best friends. It really did sound good when I pitched the idea to my parents, and in theory, I wholeheartedly thought it would work, but I was wrong again, big time.

Now here are some positives, we did split bills 50/50, and I never ever had a problem with him paying his portion of the bills, and I also was somewhat decently no longer living paycheck to paycheck. For the first time in my financial life, I was in the green, not blowing money and not necessarily saving a lot either. I can say that I was breaking even.

I had a steady girlfriend at the time, so there was no spending crazy money on multiple women going on dates. Eventually, my roommate moved out, and I ended up getting a one-bedroom apartment in the same apartment complex on the access road off Jimmy Carter Blvd. It was a great move for the sake of peace of mind, but do you see financial issues brewing?

I will say that a huge takeaway from working in collections in my college years did teach me not to get credit cards because I knew I didn't have the fortitude to not max them out. Because the last thing I needed was to be horrible at managing money and have credit card burdens. And I learned a lot about credit. A funny thing was that I did not establish credit either, so I was basically invisible in the credit world. I eventually got it together. Stick around, and you'll see.

In my new 1-bedroom apartment, all bills were back on my shoulders, and I had a newfound appreciation for my bills, my space, and my freedom. One thing I learned from having a roommate is that 2 captains will sink a ship. That experience did wake me up a bit, and I no longer blew all of my money living for the weekend. As my grandfather would so eloquently say, it's a bad wind that doesn't change.

COMPUCREDIT AND THE MAN WHO CHANGED EVERYTHING

AT my new collection job, I was collecting on charged-off mortgages. This was a bit tougher mountain to climb, but it offered a bigger payout and bonus structure. I was up for the challenge. One thing I've always been very good at is talking people into doing things they didn't necessarily want to do initially. A blessing and a curse.

I will admit that I learned quite a bit about finances from my girlfriend at the time, who was attending school for Accounting. She was masterful with money management. I eventually was fired from this really great collection agency for the same reason, not wanting to listen to my managers and thinking that I knew everything when, ultimately, I didn't know a darn thing.

I also learned a great deal in college about managing books from a company standpoint, but I never really applied my school lessons to my personal financial life. Hard times eventually came back, and I was living paycheck to paycheck. In my boring times, I'd think spending money would make me feel better. Yes, I was an emotional impulse spender, and unfortunately, this behavior lasted for years to come.

I still loved to travel and hang out with so-called friends. I say so-called because I did the majority of the traveling back to North Carolina to hang out with them, and rarely would they come to Georgia and hang out with me. This is why I said so-called, because I looked back and those relationships were one-sided, and I was the one burning up the highway, spending money on gas that I knew I should have been saving for upcoming bills. Are you gaining a clearer picture of the financial heart attack on the horizon?

I eventually moved after my lease was up to a new apartment in Doraville, GA. At this time, it was a bit more expensive, but a typical person who knew how to manage money. Long gone were the days of a $400 rent. I always felt that if I had the money to buy whatever I wanted at the moment, it would be a disservice to myself if I didn't treat myself to it. It was as if I didn't make the purchase; a part of my being would suffer in some capacity.

My parents would bail me out from time to time. Most times, I would go without just out of being embarrassed that I'd blow my check on things that didn't matter or have any type of value or give any return. I will say that at my new collection agency called CompuCredit, it was probably one of the jobs I held longest in all of the years I worked for someone else. I honestly don't know how I managed to stay there for so long. I was really cool with management, and I was very skillful at the art of collecting on bad debt.

This is where I met a gentleman named Craig R. He was a cool older guy, had a nice car, and was always a sharp dresser. But more importantly, Craig was financially free. Not rich. Not wealthy in the traditional sense. But free. He didn't stress about bills. He didn't live paycheck to paycheck. He didn't borrow from friends and family. He had peace.

I remember one day at lunch, we got to talking about money. I was probably complaining about something, bills or expenses, or whatever excuse I had that week. Craig just looked at me and said something I'll never forget: 'Young man, you're going to have a financial heart attack if you don't change your ways.'

I laughed it off at first. 'Man, I'm only 22, 23 years old, I got time.' He didn't laugh with me. He just stared and said, 'That's exactly what

I said at 22. You know how old I was when I finally got it together? 41. You know how much money I lost between 22 and 41? You don't want to know.'

Craig started breaking down his story about how he was just like me. Good job, good income, terrible with money. How he thought he had time. How he thought it would all work out. How he woke up at 39 years old with nothing. No savings. No investments. No retirement. No backup plan. Nothing.

He told me about the panic attacks. About the anxiety. About the literal chest pains he'd get when bills were due, about the shame of being a grown man who couldn't afford an emergency. About the relationships he lost because of money stress. About the opportunities he missed because he was always broke.

'That's a financial heart attack,' he said. 'When your body starts breaking down from the stress of your financial situation. When you can't sleep, when you can't breathe, when you feel like you're dying because of money, that's what happens when you spend 20 years making the same mistakes over and over again.'

I sat there at that lunch table, and something in me shifted. Not all the way. Not completely. But enough to plant a seed. Craig saw it in my eyes, and he said, 'Look, I'm not going to preach to you. But I'm going to give you one piece of advice. Write this down.'

He pulled out a pen and grabbed a napkin. On that napkin, he wrote: 'Every dollar you waste today is a day of freedom you lose tomorrow.' He slid it across the table to me. I still have that napkin. It's in a frame in my office right now.

THE AWAKENING BEGINS

AFTER that conversation with Craig, I started paying attention. Not to what he was saying, necessarily, but to what he was doing. How he moved. How he spent. How he thought about money.

Craig would bring his lunch to work. Not because he was cheap. Because he was intentional, he drove a nice car, but it was 5 years old and paid off. He dressed well, but he shopped strategically. He had subscriptions to financial magazines. He talked about compound interest the way I talked about the weekend.

One day, I asked him straight up: 'Craig, how much do you have saved?' He smiled and said, 'Enough to sleep at night. That's the only number that matters.' I pressed him. 'Come on, man, give me a real number.' He leaned back in his chair and said, 'You want a real number? Here's a real number. I have enough saved that if I lost my job tomorrow, I could live my exact same lifestyle for 18 months without touching a dime of credit or asking anyone for help. That's my number. What's yours?'

I didn't have an answer. I literally couldn't answer the question. I had maybe $300 in my account. Maybe. Probably more like $200. On a good week. If I lost my job tomorrow, I'd be in ~~crisis by~~ next week. Hell, I was already in crisis, and I had a job.

That's when it hit me. I had spent my entire life from that penny candy store at age 8 to this moment at age 23, I had spent 15 years practicing poverty. Practicing being broke. Practicing emergency living. Every single dollar I'd ever made had taught me that money comes and money goes, and you just ride the wave.

But Craig was teaching me something different. Craig was showing me that money can stay. That money can grow. That money can work for you instead of you always working for money. That freedom isn't about how much you make, it's about how much you keep.

I started asking Craig more questions. He started giving me more answers. He introduced me to concepts I'd never heard of: emergency funds, automatic transfers, the 50/30/20 rule, and the difference between assets and liabilities. He gave me books to read: Rich Dad, Poor Dad; The Millionaire Next Door; and The Richest Man in Babylon.

But here's the thing about knowledge: it only works if you apply it. And here's what I learned about myself: I was great at learning. I was terrible at applying. I could read all the books in the world. I could understand all the concepts. But when Friday came, and that direct deposit hit? Old habits took over.

The weekend would call. The shoes would call. The restaurants would call. The trips would call. And I'd answer. Every single time. Because 15 years of muscle memory is stronger than 15 weeks of good intentions.

Craig could see me struggling. He could see me trying. He could see me failing. And one day, he pulled me aside and said something that changed everything: 'Stop trying to change everything at once. You didn't get here overnight; you won't get out overnight. Pick one thing. One. Thing. And master it. Then add another thing.'

THE RECKONING

I WISH I could tell you that I listened to Craig immediately. I wish I could tell you that I changed my ways right then and there. I wish I could tell you that this is where the story gets better. But that would be a lie. And this book is about truth.

The truth is, I took Craig's advice and put it in my pocket with the napkin. The truth is, I kept living the same way. The truth is, I kept making the same mistakes. The truth is, I wasn't ready. Not yet.

Because here's what nobody tells you about change: you don't change when you see the light. You change when you feel the heat. And I hadn't felt the heat yet. Not really. Sure, I'd been broke. Sure, I'd struggled. Sure, I'd have to call my parents for help. But I'd never felt true financial pain. I'd never felt what it's like when the safety net disappears.

That pain was coming. That heat was building. That reckoning was right around the corner. And when it arrived, it would make every financial mistake up to this point look like child's play.

I remember the last conversation I had with Craig before everything changed. We were leaving work, walking to the parking lot. He said, 'You know what's coming, right?' I asked him what he meant. He stopped walking and looked at me dead in the eyes: 'Life. Life is coming. Bills get bigger. Emergencies happen. Health fails. People depend on you. And when that happens, you'd better have built something to stand on because life doesn't care about your excuses. Life doesn't care that you're young. Life doesn't care that you didn't know better. Life just comes. And it's expensive.'

I nodded as I understood. But I didn't. Not really. How could I? I was 23, healthy, employed, and convinced that tomorrow would take care of itself. I had that dangerous combination of ignorance and confidence that makes young people feel invincible.

Craig shook his head and got in his car. As he pulled away, he rolled down his window and said one last thing: 'When it happens, and it will happen, remember everything I told you. And remember, it's never too late to start. But it gets more expensive every day you wait.'

I watched his taillights fade into traffic. I had no idea that would be one of the last real conversations we'd have. Six months later, Craig would leave CompuCredit for a better opportunity. We'd lose touch. But his words? His lessons? That napkin in my wallet? Those stayed with me.

And they were about to become the most valuable things I owned. Because what happened next, what I'm about to tell you in Book 2, tested every single lesson Craig tried to teach me. It revealed every single weakness in my financial foundation. It showed me exactly what happens when you build your life on sand instead of stone.

The financial heart attack was coming. And unlike my childhood allowance, unlike those penny candy runs, unlike those spring break trips, unlike every close call I'd survived so far, this one wasn't going to reset on Friday. This one was going to change everything.

Because the thing about financial heart attacks? They don't kill you quickly. They kill you slowly. One bill at a time. One missed payment at a time. One bad decision at a time. Until one day you wake up and realize that the life you're living isn't the life you wanted. It's just the life you can afford.

And I was about to learn that lesson the hard way. The expensive way. The way that would cost me thousands of dollars and years of my life. The way that would force me to finally, finally, do what Craig had been begging me to do: change.

But that change? That transformation? That redemption? That's Book 2. And it's a story worth waiting for. Because if Book 1 is about how to have a financial heart attack, Book 2 is about how to survive it. How to recover from it. And how to make sure you never have another one.

This is where we leave off. Standing in that parking lot. Twenty-three years old. Broke. Educated but ignorant. Warned but unprepared. On the edge of the cliff, about to jump, convinced I can fly.

The question isn't whether I'll fall. The question is whether I'll learn to land. And whether I'll get back up. That's Book 2. That's the real story. That's where the heart attack happens and where the healing begins.

But before we get there, let me ask you something. As you've read this story, have you seen yourself in it? Have you recognized the patterns? Have you felt that uncomfortable recognition that maybe, just maybe, you're building the same foundation I built? Made of the same material? Sand instead of stone?

If so, here's my gift to you: you don't have to wait for the heart attack. You can change now. You can learn from my mistakes instead of making your own. You can listen to Craig's words before life forces you to. Because trust me, learning from someone else's pain is a lot cheaper than paying for your own.

Remember that napkin? 'Every dollar you waste today is a day of freedom you lose tomorrow.' That's not just advice. That's prophecy. And in Book 2, you'll see exactly how that prophecy comes true, how those wasted dollars add up. How those lost days of freedom compound into years of bondage.

See you in Book 2, where the real financial heart attack happens. And where, by God's grace and a lot of hard lessons, we learn how to survive it.

www.ingramcontent.com/pod-product-compliance
Lightning Source LLC
LaVergne TN
LVHW010739061126
851857LV00014B/1567